INSIDE:

MONTGOMERY COUNTY PARKS

PARKS NEARBY

Montgomery County Parks

CENTRAL PERKIOMEN VALLEY PARK

THE PARK:
> Central Perkiomen Valley Park is made up of over 30 parcels of woodlands, open grass and wetlands hopscotching from Collegeville to Perkiomenville.

WALKS:
> There are two walks at the 55-acre park headquarters on Plank Road. The pedestrian trail serpentines along the Perkiomen Creek, although there aren't many water views once you leave the bridge area. An old Reading Railroad right-of-way has been converted into a trail along Plank Road.

TRAIL TIME?
> Less than an hour.

TRAIL TERRAIN?
> The trails here make for very easy walking.

TRAIL SURFACE?
> These trails are all very rocky under paw.

TRAIL SENSE?
> The creekside walk is well-marked; even to the point of seeing one blaze ahead in spots - rare in Montgomery County. There is no map nor signage available; the trailhead is behind the parking lot.

> ## BONUS
> Along the creekside trail, your dog can actually walk through an old - but still vibrant - sycamore tree. You may be able to squeeze through as well, but if not you can at least walk in and gaze up into the hollow giant.

SWIMMING?
The Perkiomen Creek is wide but shallow. You can see the water depth by markings on the bridge support in the creek.

ADMISSION FEE:
None.

PARK HOURS/PHONE:
8:00 a.m. - sunset. (610.287.6970)

DIRECTIONS:
The park headquarters is on Plank Road between Gravel Pike (Route 29) and Skippack Pike (Route 73).

No Dogs!

1. Alverthorpe Park
2. Briar Bush Nature Center
3. Lorimer County Park
4. Mill Grove/Audubon Wildlife Sanctuary
5. Upper Schuylkill Valley Park

CURTIS ARBORETUM

THE PARK:

Cyrus H.K. Curtis, a 33-year old Maine native, started an 8-page folio called *The Ladies Home Journal* in Philadelphia in 1883. It was a success and in 1897 he paid $1000 for a bland 16-page weekly with a readership of less than 2300 and advertising income of only $7000 a year. By 1909 more than one million people were buying *The Saturday Evening Post* every week. The one-time publisher of the *Philadelphia Inquirer* lived on these grounds in an elegant mansion known as "Lyndon." Curtis eventually built his estate to 180 acres, including a private 18-hole golf course. After his death in 1933, the mansion was razed for tax purposes and within a decade most of the property sold off for a housing development.

A 43-acre parcel was preserved as a gift to Cheltenham Township. Although the current budget allows for little more than grass-cutting, hundreds of the spectacular trees, imported by Cyrus Curtis from around the world, remain.

WALKS:

There are no formal trails through Curtis Arboretum but the former estate grounds are ideal for romping with your dog.

TRAIL TIME?

Less than one hour.

TRAIL TERRAIN?

The arboretum flows down a hillside.

TRAIL SURFACE?

Grass, although you can walk on paved driveways and informal dirt paths if it is wet.

TRAIL SENSE?

The Curtis Arboretum is where you can let your imagination off the leash.

SWIMMING?

Two small ornamental ponds are an ideal spot for a dip.

ADMISSION FEE:

None.

PARK HOURS:

May-August, 8:00 a.m. - 8:30 p.m.;
September-April, 8:00 a.m. - 6:00 p.m.

DIRECTIONS:

Curtis Arboretum is in Wyncote. The entrance is on Church Road, just north of Township Line Road (Route 73).

How To Pet A Dog

Tickling tummies slowly and gently works wonders. Never use a rubbing motion; this makes dogs bad-tempered. A gentle tickle with the tips of the fingers is all that is necessary to induce calm in a dog. I hate strangers who go up to dogs with their hands held to the dog's nose, usually palm towards themselves. How does the dog know that the hand doesn't hold something horrid? The palm should always be shown to the dog and go straight down to between the dog's front legs and tickle gently with a soothing voice to acompany the action. Very often the dog raises its back leg in a scratching movement, it gets so much pleasure from this.

-Barbara Woodhouse

EVANSBURG STATE PARK

THE PARK:
>   This land was part of William Penn's American Province
>   purchased from the Lenni Lenape Nation in 1684. The area
>   developed rapidly; by 1714 settlers were sending goods
>   to Philadelphia via the Skippack (from the Lenape word for
>   "wetland") Pike. The agrarian ways of the Mennonites in
>   the Skippack Valley began to evaporate in the years
>   following World War II and plans began for setting aside
>   the land that became Evansburg State Park. The park
>   officially opened for public use on June 28, 1974.

WALKS:
>   Although Evansburg comprises more than 3,000 acres, most
>   of the property is set aside for hunting and trapping.
>   There are 6 miles of hiking trails, primarily on the Skippack
>   Creek Loop Trail which is essentially two linear trails on
>   either side of the Skippack Creek. On the Main Park Area
>   side the trail is wider and flatter, the far side is woodsier
>   and more scenic. Another 15 miles of walking is available
>   on equestrian trails.

TRAIL TIME?
>   More than an hour.

TRAIL TERRAIN?
>   This is mostly easy walking with some moderate ups and
>   downs, although the trail on the far side of the Skippack
>   Creek can rise some 100 feet above the water.

TRAIL SURFACE?
>   Dirt.

TRAIL SENSE?
>   The trails are blazed and a trail map is available but
>   the Skippack Loop never leaves the creek for more than
>   a few yards.

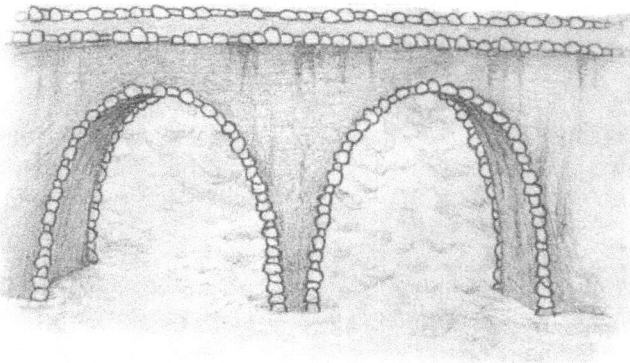

SWIMMING?

The Skippack Creek is seldom deep enough for sustained dog-paddling and there are no ponds in the park.

ADMISSION FEE:

None.

PARK HOURS/PHONE:

8:00 a.m.-sunset, year round. (610.409.1150)

DIRECTIONS:

Evansburg State Park is east of Collegeville. From Route 29, pick up Germantown Pike across the Perkiomen Bridge. Make a left on Skippack Creek Road; continue straight onto May Hill Road into the Main Park Area.

FORT WASHINGTON STATE PARK

THE PARK:

The 493-acre park is named for a defensive redoubt built by George Washington in the Fall of 1777. After being whipped at Germantown, Washington brought his 12,000 troops to this area on November 2 to regroup as he pondered whether to attack the British in Philadelphia. After five weeks, the General decided against an offensive assault and the British concluded the Americans had prepared their defenses too well to be attacked. Washington ended the stalemate by marching the Continental Army 15 miles to Valley Forge for the winter.

In the early 1920s, Philadelphia's Fairmount Park Commission began acquiring land here, even though it lay outside the city limits. In 1953, the Commission turned the park over to the Commonwealth of Pennsylvania.

WALKS:

There are 3.5 miles of wooded trails at Fort Washington, primarily in the Militia Hill Day Use Area. The interlocking trails, many on old vehicle roads, can be combined to form loop walks. None, however, escape the constant drone of traffic on the nearby Pennsylvania Turnpike. A segment of the Green Ribbon Trail passes through the park, connecting the Militia Hill and Flourtown areas.

TRAIL TIME?

Less than one hour.

TRAIL TERRAIN?

The trails across Joshua Road are hilly; the cross-country trail that circumnavigates the picnic area is less so.

TRAIL SURFACE?

The old vehicle roads are stony and overgrown with grass; the cross-country trail is grass and dirt.

TRAIL SENSE?

The trails are not marked but an accurate park map is available.

SWIMMING?

There is access to a deep stretch of the Wissahickon Creek along the Green Ribbon Trail at the edge of the park. There is no water anywhere else.

ADMISSION FEE:

None.

PARK HOURS:

Sunrise - sunset, year-round.

DIRECTIONS:

Fort Washington State Park lies between Fort Washington and Flourtown, two miles from the Pennsylvania Turnpike, Exit 26. To reach the Militia Hill Day Use Area, take Skippack Pike (Route 73) and turn onto Joshua Road to the entrance on the left.

FOUR MILLS NATURE RESERVE

THE PARK:

The Four Mills Nature Reserve comprises 55 acres of Wissahickon Creek floodplain, 50 of which were donated by former Philadelphia *Bulletin* owner, Robert McLean, in 1966. The original estate named Abendruh, German for "evening's rest," was created by Charles Bergner of Bergner and Engle Brewing Company, a 19th century Philadelphia brewery. McLean used the estate as a private hunting ground, stocking the property with pheasant and quail. Four Mills derives its name from four long-disappeared mills that once operated in the vicinity.

WALKS:

The trails at Four Mills lie on islands in the Wissahickon Creek (if your dog shies away from open-grate bridges, you may have to carry him). As of this writing, storm damage had decimated some of the downstream trails. You can also access the Green Ribbon Trail here, including Tall Tree Woods. A good walk at Four Mills is to take the Green Ribbon Trail between water crossings upstream and downstream.

TRAIL TIME?

Less than one hour.

TRAIL TERRAIN?

Flat.

TRAIL SURFACE?

The trails are mostly soft dirt with some stony stretches.

TRAIL SENSE?

A trail map and mapboard in the parking lot point out the available trails; all of which are short and interlocking.

SWIMMING?

The normal level of the Wissahickon is not deep enough for dog paddling.

ADMISSION FEE:
  None.

PARK HOURS/PHONE:
  Dawn to dusk. (215.646.8866)

DIRECTIONS:
  Four Mills Nature Reserve is just south of Ambler at
  12 Morris Road, east of Butler Pike.

Best Parks To Take
The Dog Swimming

1. Green Lane Park

2. Skymount Open Space

3. Schuylkill Canal Park

4. Valley Forge National Historical Park

5. Central Perkiomen Valley Park

GRAEME PARK

THE PARK:
> Graeme Park was built on 1200 acres in 1722 as the summer residence for the Provincial Governor of Pennsylvania, Sir William Keith. Keith would later tangle with the still powerful Penn family, be removed from office, return to England and die. His son-in-law, Dr. Thomas Graeme, purchased the property in 1734 and the country retreat remained in the Graeme family until 1801. Passed through several families thereafter, it was conveyed to the Commonwealth of Pennsylvania in 1958.

WALKS:
> Graeme Park features a 3/4-mile Nature Trail. Each of the 17 stops on the self-guided tour has been selected for its relevance to Colonial life in rural America.

TRAIL TIME?
> Less than an hour.

TRAIL TERRAIN?
> Flat.

TRAIL SURFACE?
> Grass, with dirt paths along Park Creek. The surface is so gentle, the park feels the need to recommend the wearing of shoes.

TRAIL SENSE?
> The Nature Trail is a loop marked by numbered posts. A rudimentary trail map is available.

SWIMMING?
> Park Creek is suitable only for doggie splashing.

ADMISSION FEE:
> None.

PARK HOURS/PHONE:
> Daily, 10:00 a.m. - 4:00 p.m. (215.343.0965)

DIRECTIONS:

Graeme Park is located in Horsham Township, at the corner of Keith Valley Road and County Line Road. The entrance is on County Line Road, just west of the intersection with Easton Road (Route 611).

Ever consider what they must think of us? I mean, here we come back from the grocery store with the most amazing haul - chicken, pork, half a cow...They must think we're the greatest hunters on earth!

-Anne Tyler

15

GREEN LANE PARK

THE PARK:

Public recreation here dates to 1939 with the founding of Upper Perkiomen Valley Park. With its wedding to Green Lane Reservoir Park, the largest single open space purchase-easement in Montgomery County history, Green Lane Park was created. The focal point of the 3100-acre park is the Green Lane Reservoir, home to more than a dozen species of freshwater fish.

WALKS:

Four of the five trails here are open to dogs (four-legged friends are not welcome on the Hemlock Point Trail). The Red Trail winds through open fields and stands of trees for 10 miles, although the entire length can be aborted in several places. The marquee trail at Green Lane Park is the heavily wooded Blue Trail on the western edge of the reservoir where you pick your way across steep ravines and narrow ridges for 6 miles. The full loop can be cut off at the Turn Around but you'll miss the extravagant rock carvings of falling water at work. At the Hill Road Office, and overlapping the Blue Trail, is the Whitetail Trail, a self-guided nature walk. The Orange Trail is a two-mile loop in the Deep Lake vicinity.

TRAIL TIME?

More than an hour.

TRAIL TERRAIN?

There are hilly climbs throughout Green Lane Park; the gentlest terrain is found on the Red Trail.

TRAIL SURFACE?

Grass, especially on the Red Trail, and dirt; there are stretches of loose rocks on the Blue Trail.

```
┌─────────────────────────────────────────────┐
│                   BONUS                       │
│  On the Red Trail, there is an unexpected walk│
│ into a young stand of cedar growing on red dirt│
│      and the feeling of Utah desert instantly │
│                washes over you.               │
└─────────────────────────────────────────────┘
```

TRAIL SENSE?

A good trail map is available - and do not let go of it. The trails are blazed, but not energetically. The Red Trail uses ribbons which are sometimes tied to fallen posts. Among the things NOT to try at Green Lane: following the Orange Trail from the parking lot as indicated on the map (it is not marked) and trying the Red Trail clockwise (there is a reason the map uses directional arrows).

SWIMMING?

There is excellent access to the reservoir from the Blue Trail; less so on the Red Trail.

ADMISSION FEE:

None.

PARK HOURS/PHONE:

6:00 a.m. - sunset, year-round. (215.234.8684)

DIRECTIONS:

Green Lane Park is in northwestern Montgomery County. Heading north on Route 29 there are several approaches to the trails. For the Orange Trail, make a left on Snyder Road, drive through the recreation area to the parking lot on Deep Creek Road. For the Blue Trail, make a left on Park Road and a right on Hill Road to the trailhead on the left. The Red Trail is just off Route 29 on Knight Road.

Dogs' lives are too short. Their only fault, really.
-Agnes Sligh Turnbull

GREEN RIBBON TRAIL

THE PARK:

The name "Wissahickon" is rooted in two words from the Lenni-Lenape nation, the original settlers in the area: *Wissahickon*, or "yellow colored stream" and *Wisamickan*, or "catfish creek." German settlers began arriving in 1683 and by 1756 the Lenape Indians had been pushed from the area by the industrious immigrants. In the next hundred years the Wissahickon Creek, whose flow was much stronger centuries ago, would support 54 mills. This over-development sapped the power from the creek and fouled its waters.

The non-profit Wissahickon Valley Watershed Association formed in 1957 to resurrect and protect the historic creek. The Wissahickon Green Ribbon Preserve Trail created by the activists stretches almost unbroken for 21 miles from Lansdale to the Schuylkill River in Philadelphia.

WALKS:

The Green Ribbon Trail is a linear trail along the length of Wissahickon Creek. Due to two unbreechable parcels of private land, the Ribbon is essentially three segments. The downstream segement is the Forbidden Drive through the Wissahickon Gorge in Fairmount Park. The middle leg is a wooded band from Whitemarsh to Ambler. The Green Ribbon gets less wooded in its northern stretches from Penllyn to North Wales. The trail moves from bank to bank without bridges and requires streamwalking in places.

TRAIL TIME?

More than an hour.

TRAIL TERRAIN?

Before the Wissahickon reaches the Gorge the trail is flat and virtually always at creek level.

TRAIL SURFACE?

Mostly dirt, although you can encounter almost anything here.

TRAIL SENSE?

The Wissahickon Valley Watershed Association sells a map of the Green Ribbon Trail for $1.00, which is money well spent if any extended walking is planned as it identifies where the trail switches sides of the creek. The trailheads at public roads are marked by signposts and the trail is marked by green blazes.

SWIMMING?

The deeper swimming holes are more downstream than upstream.

ADMISSION FEE:

None.

PARK HOURS:

Dawn to dusk.

DIRECTIONS:

There is access to the Green Ribbon Trail anywhere it crosses a public road. Parking is not always available near these junctions, however. Some parking locations, from north to south, are Evans-Mumbower Mill on Swedesford Road at Township Line Road; at the Nature Area on Penllyn Pike at Lantern Lane; the Four Mills Nature Reserve at 12 Morris Road in Ambler; and on the Skippack Pike (Route 73) west of Bethelhem Pike.

GWYNEDD WILDLIFE PRESERVE

THE PARK:

The land here was farmed until 1986 when it was acquired by the Natural Lands Trust. The preserve features 180 acres of meadows and 40 acres of woodlands, half of which is not open to the public.

WALKS:

Most of the four miles of these wide, well-maintained trails traverse the meadowlands. Only a short end of the Buck Run Trail visits the woodlands and it is narrow and muddy in wet weather. The trails do not loop but there are enough of them and they intersect often so it is easy to chart a non-repetitive walk. The many house views and power lines are reminders why these preserves are necesssary.

TRAIL TIME?

More than an hour.

TRAIL TERRAIN?

This is easy walking over rolling topography that has an elevation rise of about 80 feet.

TRAIL SURFACE?
Mostly grass.

TRAIL SENSE?
A detailed trail map is available and signposts mark
intersections. This is some of the best open field walking
in Montgomery County and it is easy to see where you are.

SWIMMING?
There are two wetland ponds on the property. The more
whimsical of the two features gum drop islands that can be
reached by land bridges in drier times.

ADMISSION FEE:
None.

PARK HOURS/PHONE:
Gates close at 4:00 p.m. (215.699.6751)

DIRECTIONS:
From the intersection of Route 202 and Route 73 head
north on Route 202 past Montgomery County Community
College and the light at Morris Road. Take the next left
onto Township Line Road and make the first right onto
Swedesford Road. The preserve entrance is 1/2 mile on
the left.

*If you pick up a starving dog and make him prosperous, he
will not bite you. This is the principal difference between a
dog and a man.*
                                        -Mark Twain

LOWER PERKIOMEN VALLEY
COUNTY PARK

THE PARK:
> There is just enough copper in the ground along the Perkiomen Creek to have sparked dreams in early fortune hunters . Lead mines were worked across the creek from the park in Mill Grove but never with much luck. In January of 1848 the elusive copper was discovered there. By 1851 investors had pooled $300,000 to form the Perkiomen Mining Association. Shafts were dug over 300 feet into the ground. But there was never enough copper. Over the next few years 525 tons of copper were dragged to the surface but the good quality ore fetched only $30,575. The venture was abandoned in 1858.
>
> The Lower Perkiomen Valley Park, on the banks of the Perkiomen Creek, just upstream from its confluence with the Schuylkill River, is a popular picnic spot.

WALKS:
> Dogs are not allowed in the picnic area but there are 30 acres of open multi-use fields in which dogs can romp. There are no formal trails here.

TRAIL TIME?
> Less than an hour.

TRAIL TERRAIN?
> This floodplain area is flat.

TRAIL SURFACE?
> Grass.

TRAIL SENSE?
> No need to funnel down pre-determined chutes of trail like doomed cattle here.

SWIMMING?

There is access to the deep Perkiomen Creek above the dam here.

ADMISSION FEE:

None.

PARK HOURS/PHONE:

8:00 a.m. - sunset, year-round.

DIRECTIONS:

Lower Perkiomen Valley Park is in Upper Providence Township. From Route 422, take the Oaks/Audubon interchange towards Audubon. Make an immediate right onto New Mill Road to the park entrance on the left. Parking for the open fields is along the road before the entrance.

Best Parks To Hike More Than An Hour With The Dog

1. Green Lane Park

2. Valley Forge National Historical Park

3. Evansburg State Park

4. Norristown Farm Park

5. Pennypack Preserve

MAIN LINE COLLEGES

THE PARK:

> When school is not in session, there are few better walks than around a deserted college campus. Several private colleges along the Main Line welcome responsible dog owners to visit campus.

WALKS:

> *Bryn Mawr College Arboretum.* This English-landscape-style campus mixes massive trees with its Gothic buildings. The campus grounds were designed by the firm of Frederick Law Olmstead, architects of many of America's greatest parks.

> *Haverford College Arboretum.* Once the center of the Welsh Tract, a prominent group of Quakers purchased 198.5 acres here in 1831. Two years later Haverford College was founded, making it the oldest institution of higher learning with Quaker roots in the country. There are two walking choices here: a nearly three-mile loop around the perimeter of the campus (you'll barely see any buildings) or an Arboretum tour highlighting 33 special trees.

> *Rosemont College.* At 56 acres, the smallest of the Main Line grounds, Rosemont offers a quiet walk around the knob of a hill. At the center of campus is Rathalla, resplendent with its French Renaissance turrets. The original house on the Sinnott Estate, it once contained all college activities.

> *Villanova Arboretum.* The oldest and largest Catholic university in Pennsylvania formally dedicated its arboretum in 1993 - more than 100 years after many of the school's 1,500 trees were well-established. The trees are easily identified from the paths.

TRAIL TIME?

> Less than an hour; although you can spend more than an hour at Haverford on the Nature Trail.

TRAIL TERRAIN?

It is easy walking through all the colleges.

TRAIL SURFACE?

Most of the time is spent on paved walkways although the Nature Trail at Haverford is dirt.

TRAIL SENSE?

Bryn Mawr, Haverford and Villanova have numerous map boards. The only formal trail is at Haverford and is actually 3/4 of a loop which must be completed by ducking through some back parking lots; a campus map and brochure are available.

SWIMMING?

There are small streams at Haverford and Rosemont but no canine swimming on campus.

ADMISSION FEE:

None.

PARK HOURS:

Dawn to Dusk.

DIRECTIONS:

From East to West: Haverford is on Route 30. Follow the signs to the Visitor Parking Lot where you can pick up a campus map and the trailhead. Bryn Mawr is three blocks north of Route 30 via Roberts Road. Parking is on the street. Rosemont College is on Montgomery Avenue; visitor parking is to the left of the entrance. Villanova is spread across Routes 30 and 320. The main parking lot is opposite the campus on Route 30.

MCKAIG NATURE EDUCATION CENTER

THE PARK:

The Upper Merion Park and Historic Foundation was created in 1964 to preserve the area's rapidly diminishing open space. Small accruals of land gifts began accumulating and today the McKaig Nature Education Center pushes back the encroaching development with 89 wooded acres.

WALKS:

Three wide and well-maintained trails range in walking time from 15 minutes to 45 minutes. The Cadet Trail is a linear exploration running up the spine of the property. Two loop trails branch off the Cadet: the Nancy Long Trail and the short, but steep Laurel Trail.

TRAIL TIME?

Less than an hour.

TRAIL TERRAIN?

The loops are hillier than the Cadet Trail but the trails work around the hillside rather than straight up the slopes on these sporty walks.

TRAIL SURFACE?

Dirt; at times embedded with stones.

TRAIL SENSE?

The Cadet Trail (white blazes) and the Nancy Long Trail (yellow blazes) are well-marked. The Laurel Trail is unmarked; look for the entrance under a fallen tree. A trail map is available at the trailhead.

SWIMMING?

The Crow Creek is a tumbling, pleasing little brook but seldom deep enough for anything beyond doggie splashing.

ADMISSION FEE:
None.

PARK HOURS:
Dawn to dusk.

DIRECTIONS:
McKaig Nature Education Center is bounded roughly by King of Prussia Road, Brower Road and Croton Road. Parking is available on Brower Road (one or two cars on the roadside) and at the Roberts School on Croton Road. From Route 202, take Warner Road south to the end. Make a left on Croton road and the school is on the right.

NORRISTOWN FARM PARK

THE PARK:

The area that is today Norristown Farm Park was part of a 7000-acre tract of land belonging to William Penn, known as "Williamstadt." The ownership of the Norris family dates to October 10, 1704 when Penn's son sold the land to Isaac Norris and William Trent for the hefty sum of 850 pounds. On November 11, 1717, Trent sold his share of the manor to Norris.

After many subsequent lords, in 1876 the Pennsylvania legislature authorized the purchase of the manor for the Norristown State Hospital. The hospital eventually spread across 981 acres, 831 of which became a farm supplying not only food but a supposed conduit to patient recovery. Farm operations became too costly and ceased in 1975 and the farm fell into disrepair. In 1992, Montgomery County leased 690 acres to create the county's second largest park.

WALKS:

There are wide, multi-use trails totalling more than five miles at Norristown Farm Park. The trails roughly combine to form adjacent loops in a figure-eight pattern, passing through natural areas and cultivated fields of the revitalized farm where corn, soybeans and winter grains grow. There are long periods without shade.

TRAIL TIME:
> More than an hour.

TRAIL TERRAIN?
> The walking is easy across these rolling hills.

TRAIL SURFACE?
> All the trails are paved in macadam.

TRAIL SENSE?
> A detailed trail map is available at the Milk House Visitor
> Center and is posted on boards in the parking lot.

SWIMMING?
> Two branches of Stony Creek knife through the property
> before joining at the baseball field into one stream.
> Although reaching a swimming-friendly depth of four feet
> in places, the water is only accessed by the trail a few
> times.

ADMISSION FEE:
> None.

PARK HOURS/PHONE:
> Dawn to dusk. (610.270.0215)

DIRECTIONS:
> Norristown Farm Park is in northwestern Norristown.
> The main entrance is off Germantown Pike on Upper Farm
> Road (the first house on the right along the entrance road
> is Shannon Mansion, built in 1764 and the oldest building
> on the property). There is also parking on Whitehall Road.

PENNYPACK PRESERVE

THE PARK:
> The privately owned Pennypack Ecological Restoration Trust has been assembling a natural area preserve since 1970. Using land purchases, donations and conservation easements, the preserve has grown to 683 acres.

WALKS:
> There are 7 miles of trails here; dogs are allowed only in the Wilderness Area. Three connecting trails, each with its own personality, create a linear trail along the Pennypack Creek for about 2 1/2 miles. The longest, the Creek Road Trail, is a country lane walk with plenty of access to the meandering stream. The middle leg, the Pennpack Creek Trail, hugs a hillside and is characterized by tall trees, especially conifers. The Pennypack Parkway is an old access road, draped in a shaded canopy of trees.

TRAIL TIME?
> More than an hour.

TRAIL TERRAIN?
> Mostly flat with imperceptible ups and downs.

TRAIL SURFACE?
> The Deep Creek Road Trail is comprised of macadam, stones and dirt; Pennypack Creek Trail is mostly dirt; and the Pennypack Parkway is gravel.

TRAIL SENSE?
> There are signposts and a trail map is available at the trailhead. Do not take any of the spur trails as they lead into the Environmental Management Center where dogs are not allowed.

SWIMMING?
> The Pennypack Creek is seldom more than two feet deep, save for the base of Huntingdon Road where there are deep pools for doggie paddling.

ADMISSION FEE:
> None.

PARK HOURS/PHONE:
> Dawn to dusk. (215.657.0830)

DIRECTIONS:
> The Pennypack Preserve is on the western edge of
> Bryn Athyn; the trailhead for the wilderness trails is at
> the corner of Terwood Road and Creek Road. From the
> intersection of Huntingdon Pike (Route 232) and Old Welsh
> Road (Route 63), go west on Old Welsh Road and make
> the first right across the bridge onto Terwood Road.
> Creek Road is one mile on the right. The trails can also
> be accessed from Mason's Mill Park on Mason's Mill Road.

RIVERBEND ENVIRONMENTAL EDUCATION CENTER

THE PARK:
The Riverbend story begins 300,000,000 years ago when a crack in the rock known as the Rosemont Fault turned what would become known as the Schuylkill River a full 90 degrees. The first settlers came to the area in the 1500s when the Lenni-Lenape Indians began planting vegetables in an area known as 'Indian Fields." In 1904, Howard Wood, brother of steel magnate Alan Wood, created a 52-acre farm inside the river's elbow. Three generations later, in 1974, his descendents deeded half of the farm to serve as a wildlife refuge known as Riverbend Environmental Education Center.

WALKS:
The feature trail at Riverbend, amidst two miles of hiking, is the Aloha Trail which circles the perimeter of the property. Unfortunately the walk is marred by the relentless pounding of traffic on the Schuylkill Expressway below. Look for Fiveleaf Akebia, an invasive plant which covers everything on the hillside above the roadway. The other trails are short connecting spurs of only several minutes duration. Avoid the Jack-in-the-Pulpit and Poplar Trails, which are overgrown. Another hike here is Sid Thayer's Trail, a linear trail on private property which is also plagued by traffic noise.

TRAIL TIME:
More than an hour if you hike the Sid Thayer's Trail.

TRAIL TERRAIN?
Riverbend is situated on the knob of a hill and there is little flat walking to be had here.

TRAIL SURFACE?
Dirt and grass .

BONUS

The Visitor Center is a restoration of a 1923 Sears & Roebuck mail order barn. A century ago Sears sold anything and everything by mail - including kits for building houses and barns. The kit, which could cost as little as a few hundred dollars depending on style, would include rough lumber, framing timbers, plank flooring, shingles, hardware, sash and paint. Usually shipped by train from the west, the barn kit would be loaded onto a freight wagon and hauled to the building site for assembly by local carpenters.

TRAIL SENSE?

There is a hand-painted mapboard at the parking lot for orientation. On the trails there are signposts at junctions. The Aloha Trail is blazed in red and marked by trail signs which are handy through the tricky residential passage.

SWIMMING?

Riverbend sports the smallest pond in the tri-state area, alongside the Bluebird Trail. Although scarcely ten feet across, smaller dogs can motor around and larger ones can drop in to cool off.

ADMISSION FEE:

None.

PARK HOURS/PHONE:

Sunrise - sunset, year-round. (610.527.5234)

DIRECTIONS:

Riverbend is in Lower Merion Township. From the Blue Route (I-476) North, take Exit 6A for Conshohocken, Route 23 East. Make a left on Spring Mill Road, continue past the Philadelphia Country Club and bear left at the end of the road to the Education Center parking lot.

RIVERFRONT PARK

THE PARK:

Pottstown was founded on the banks of the Schuylkill River in 1752 by ironmaster John Potts. He surveyed and laid out the first town in Montgomery County, placing the streets at right angles and in line with High Street or Main Street as William Penn had done in Philadelphia. While industrial concerns made possible by the advance of the Philadelphia & Reading Railroad long ago seized most of the waterfront, 11 acres have been reclaimed for Riverfront Park.

WALKS:

Riverfront Park features a 3/4 mile multi-use trail along the river. Unlike longer such trails, the pace here is more leisurely and well-suited for dog walking.

Across the river in Chester County's River Park is an unmaintained trail which also parallels the Schuylkill River.

TRAIL TIME?

Less than one hour.

TRAIL TERRAIN?

These waterside trails are flat.

TRAIL SURFACE?

The Riverfront Park trail is paved and includes wooden boardwalk bridges. The River Park trail is dirt; mud in wet times.

TRAIL SENSE?

Neither of these linear trails is marked, but never do you stray far from the water.

SWIMMING?

There is abundant access to the Schuylkill River here.

ADMISSION FEE:

None.

PARK HOURS:

Sunrise - sunset, year-round.

DIRECTIONS:

The parking lot for Riverfront Park is on the river side of the Industrial Highway, west of Hanover Street. To get to River Park, cross the Schuylkill River and make the first right on River Road, which runs through River Park.

My dog can bark like a Congressman, fetch like an aide, beg like a press secretary and play dead like a receptionist.
-Gerald Solomon

ROLLING HILL PARK

THE PARK:

In the early 1990s, a small band of like-minded conservationists began gathering in a church basement to plot the preservation of Lower Merion's natural areas. In 1994, the local activists convinced the township to purchase the former Walter C. Pew estate and convert the 103-acre property into Rolling Hill Park. More than 900 area families donated money to create this new park, home of the Lower Merion Conservancy.

WALKS:

The trails at Rolling Hill criss-cross over a large slope of the Mill Creek valley. The trails, some of which also serve as a steeplechase practice site, are generally wide. The park is heavily wooded with patches of open pasture.

TRAIL TIME?

More than an hour.

TRAIL TERRAIN?

Hilly, including some long climbs. There is a flat walk along Mill Creek.

TRAIL SURFACE?

Mostly dirt and grass; some stony walks.

TRAIL SENSE?

The trails are not marked, no map is available and there is no discernible trailhead. There are plans to implement formal trails and signage at Rolling Hill Park but until then, come with a mind to explore.

SWIMMING?

Mill Creek is not deep enough for canine swimming.

ADMISSION FEE:
None.

PARK HOURS:
Dawn to dusk.

DIRECTIONS:
Rolling Hill Park is in Gladwyne. From the Schuylkill Expressway (I-76), take Interchange 29 to Route 23 East. Make a left on Youngs Ford Road and a quick right on Rose Glen Road. The second right is the entrance to the park.

Any man who does not like dogs and want them does not deserve to be in the White House.

-Calvin Coolidge

SAUNDERS WOODS

THE PARK:
William Penn was intimately familiar with this section of his land grant. He personally laid out the Old Gulph Road, riding the entire distance on horseback and supervising the erection of mileposts. The boundaries of this 25-acre tract, managed by the Natural Lands Trust, have remained intact since it was subdivided from the Welsh Tract in 1792.

WALKS:
There are two miles of trails which begin in meadowland, lead into mature forests, and plunge down a steep stream valley. The trails are wide and well-maintained. Extensive plantings of native wildflowers enhance the natural surroundings.

TRAIL TIME:
Less than an hour.

TRAIL TERRAIN?
The valley slopes are severe enough to warrant a switchback trail but the majority of walking is easy.

TRAIL SURFACE?
Mown grass through the meadow, dirt in the woods.

TRAIL SENSE?
The trails are not marked and no map is available but you won't need your dog's nose to complete this pleasant walk.

SWIMMING?
The small stream heading for the Schuylkill River two miles away can be hopped across in most places.

ADMISSION FEE:
None.

PARK HOURS:
Dusk to dawn.

DIRECTIONS:

Saunders Woods is in Lower Merion Township. From Gladwyne, take Route 23 West and turn left on Waverly Road. The preserve entrance is on the right, past Scott Road.

As a young lawyer, 19th century Senator George Graham Vest of Missouri, addressed the jury on behalf of his client, suing a neighbor who had killed his dog. Vest's speech has come to be known as "Tribute to the Dog."

The best friend a man has in the world may turn against him and become his enemy. His son or daughter that he has reared with loving care may prove ungrateful. Those who are nearest and dearest to us, those whom we trust with our happiness and our good name may become traitors to their faith. The money that a man has, he may lose. It flies away from him, perhaps when he needs it most. A man's reputation may be sacrificed in a moment of ill-considered action. The people who are prone to fall on their knees to do us honor when success is with us may be the first to throw the stone of malice when failure settles its cloud upon our heads.

The one absolutely unselfish friend that man can have in this selfish world, the one that never deserts him, the one that never proves ungrateful or treacherous is his dog. A man's dog stands by him in prosperity and in poverty, in health and in sickness. He will sleep on the cold ground, where the wintry winds blow and the snow drives fiercely, if only he may be near his master's side. He will kiss the hand that has no food to offer; he will lick the wounds and sores that come in an encounter with the roughness of the world. He guards the sleep of his pauper master as if he were a prince. When all other friends desert, he remains. When riches take wings, and reputation falls to pieces, he is as constant in his love as the sun in its journey through the heavens.

If fortune drives the master forth an outcast in the world, friendless and homeless, the faithful dog asks no higher privilege than that of accompanying him, to guard him against danger, to fight against his enemies. And when the last scene of all comes, and death takes his master in its embrace and his body is laid away in the cold ground, no matter if all other friends pursue their way, there by the graveside will the noble dog be found, his head between his paws, his eyes sad, but open in alert watchfulness, faithful and true even in death.

SCHUYLKILL CANAL PARK

THE PARK:

Pennsylvania's first canal system was cobbled together in 1815 by the Schuylkill Navigation Company. The waterway, requiring 120 locks, stretched 108 miles from the coal fields of Schuylkill County to Philadelphia. Twenty-three of the locks were dug out by hand. The enterprise cost a staggering $1.8 million but was wildly successful. Investors realized dividends as high as 19% in good years when as many as 1400 boats plied the canal waters. Railroads began chewing away at canal business in the 1860s and the last coal barges floated down the Schuylkill River in the 1920s. Today, the only sections of the canal in existence are at Manayunk and Lock 60 at the Schuylkill Canal Park.

Lock 60 dates to the 1820s and the area was first named for its engineer-builder, Thomas Oakes. In 1985 the Schuylkill Canal Association formed to keep the canal flowing and maintain the lock and towpath. In 1988, the area was added to the National Register of Historic Places.

WALKS:

The peaceful towpath along the canal covers 2 1/2 miles from the Lock House, built in 1836, to the eastern end of Port Providence. The trail, which passes tall trees, low-lying wetlands and low brush, loops here for the return trip along the river. Upstream from Lock 60 are the Ravine Trail through the high rock bluffs overlooking the Schuylkill River, and the Valley View Trail, which deadends - for dogwalking - at the Upper Schuylkill Valley Park. No dogs are allowed in that park. There is also an 8-station self-guided nature walk from the Lock House to Route 29.

TRAIL TIME?

More than one hour.

TRAIL TERRAIN?

You can either enjoy the flattest walk in Montgomery County (the towpath) or the steepest (the Ravine Trail, with three ascents to 100-foot bluffs).

BONUS

Upstream from Black Rock Dam is a rocky crag which towers 100 feet over the water and carries the following 19th century lore: "A stunted cedar grew upon the very verge and it made the most masculine heart tremble to stand upon the edge and while clinging to this frail support look down into the waters beneath. Sometime after the settlement when the natives had been in contact with the whites long enough to acquire their vices an Indian was tempted with the promise of a bottle of whiskey to leap three times from this crag into the river. Twice he made the terrible plunge successfully. Returning after the second attempt wearied with the unwanted exertion and bleeding from wounds made by some sharp stones against which he had struck he sprang again into the stream never more to appear." Since that time it has borne the name of Indian Rock. Reached by trail, a hand-made wooden cross today marks the spot - "Indian's Altar."

TRAIL SURFACE?
Mostly dirt, with some rocky areas.

TRAIL SENSE?
The towpath trail is not marked, nor need it be. A trail map is available. The Ravine Trail is marked by pink ribbons.

SWIMMING?
There is great swimming in the river and the canal.

ADMISSION FEE:
None.

PARK HOURS:
Dawn to dusk

DIRECTIONS:
There is parking on either side of the Route 29 bridge and at the end of Port Providence Road in Port Providence.

SKYMOUNT OPEN SPACE

THE PARK:

    Parts of the area around Skymount Lake are maintained as open space by Marlborough Township.

WALKS:

    There is a waterside trail halfway around Skymount Lake. The trailhead is not marked; to pick it up walk down to the lake and turn right into the tall grass. CAREFUL - there are ankle-eating holes across this disheartening stretch of trail, which is mercifully short. The rest of the trail along the edge of the lake is studded with wildflowers.

TRAIL TIME?

    Less than an hour.

TRAIL TERRAIN?

    Flat.

TRAIL SURFACE?

    After the muddy beginning, the trail is grass.

TRAIL SENSE?

Once you find the trail there is no navigation work to do.

SWIMMING?

The best access to Skymount Lake is at the parking area and at the end of the trail, across the lake.

ADMISSION FEE:

None.

PARK HOURS:

Dawn to dusk.

DIRECTIONS:

Skymount Lake is in eastern Marlborough Township at the Bucks County line. From Allentown Road make a left on Ridge Road (Route 563) in Tylersport. After crossing over the Pennsylvania Turnpike make a right on White's Mill Road and then your first right on Long Road (an unmarked Gravel Road). Skymount Lake will be on your right.

STONE HILLS WILDLIFE PRESERVE

THE PARK:

Stone Hills is a tiny part of a great tract of 25,000 acres sold by William Penn to the German Company, formed by Daniel Falckner and his associates at the city of Frankfurtam Main, in Germany. This country parkland is a 13-acre refuge of the Natural Lands Trust.

WALKS:

This heavily forested preserve features quiet walks on wide trails. There is a short central loop with spurs leading to three corners of the park.

TRAIL TIME?

Less than one hour.

TRAIL TERRAIN?

The property slopes gently into the center of the woods.

TRAIL SURFACE?

After a wood chip entrance walk, the trails are dirt; the dirt can be mud in the marshy center of the preserve.

TRAIL SENSE?

The trails are not marked and no map is available but there is no danger of not finding your way back to the car.

SWIMMING?

A small stream snakes attractively through the property, good for a dog to jump into.

ADMISSION FEE:

None.

PARK HOURS:

Sunrise - sunset, year-round.

BONUS

At least in these woods, there are no hills and only some stone. The overall area, known as the Stone Hills, was the site of Pennsylvania's first copper mine and only the second mine of any sort in America. William Penn described copper discoveries along the Swamp Creek as early as 1683, although no shipments of ore were recorded until 1740. There is copper in the hills along the lower three miles of the Perkiomen Creek and it was claimed to house a finely developed vein of rich copper. So rich that prior to the American Revolution, its proprietors ordered the openings securely hidden and sealed up, "so that in case the war should be terminated disastrously, the treasure should not fall in the hands of the enemy, but lost to the world." More likely, it was not a profitable venture. The mine has been abandoned ever since.

DIRECTIONS:

Stone Hills is in Neiffer in Limerick Township. From the town of Limerick, take Ridge Pike west to Swamp Pike. Make a right on Swamp Pikeand right again on Neiffer Road. Take the second left on Laver Road and continue to the preserve parking area on the right. From Route 73, make a left on Gerloff past Zieglerville. Follow all the way to the end at Laver Road, make a left and the preserve is on the left.

The greatest pleasure of a dog is that you may make a fool of yourself with him, and not only will he not scold you, but will make a fool of himself too.

-Samuel Butler

UPPER FREDERICK OPEN SPACE

THE PARK:

This open space along Swamp Creek has been set aside by Upper Frederick Township. The Lenni Lenape Indians first settled this region and during the American Revolution Washington's Army spent time in nearby Camp Pottsgrove in September 1777 as the British occupied Philadelphia.

WALKS:

There are two markedly different linear trails here. Downstream from Colonial Road the trail is at creek-level and veers away from the water and through marshy bottomland. Along Swamp Creek grows a species of hickory bearing nuts of extraordinary size in a hard, thick shell. Across the bridge, the rugged, wooded trail hugs Swamp Creek in swales and valleys.

TRAIL TIME?

More than an hour.

TRAIL TERRAIN?

There are some steep ravines on the upstream section of the trail.

TRAIL SURFACE?

Dirt; the downstream section of the trail can be unpassable when wet.

TRAIL SENSE?

The trails are not marked but it is easy to use the Swamp Creek for orientation.

SWIMMING?

There are good swimming holes in Swamp Creek, which is generally shallow.

ADMISSION FEE:
    None.

PARK HOURS:
    Dawn to dusk.

DIRECTIONS:
    There are no signs for this open space, probably because there is no name for it. Travelling west on Route 73, make a left on Colonial Road and follow it to Swamp Creek, where the bridge is out. Park here. The downstream trail is on this side of the bridge; the upstream trail leading to the hemlock grove is across the bridge.

Money will buy a pretty good dog but it won't buy the wag of his tail.

                                                                    -Josh Billings

VALLEY FORGE NATIONAL HISTORICAL PARK

THE PARK:
>The most famous name in the American Revolution comes to us from a small iron forge built along Valley Creek in the 1740s. No battles were fought here, but during the winter of 1777-78, when Valley Forge grew to be the third largest city in America, hundreds of soldiers died from sickness and disease. America's attention was redirected to long-forgotten Valley Forge during a Centennial in 1878. Preservation efforts began with Washington's Headquarters and evolved into the National Historic Park.

WALKS:
>While the main park lies across the Schuylkill River in Chester County, there are miles of trails in Montgomery County at Walnut Hill (once the commissary for Washington's troops) and on the 3-mile linear trail connecting the Pawling's Parking Area and the Betzwood Picnic Area. In the Picnic Area, you can also pick up the Schuylkill River Trail which runs 22 miles to Philadelphia but this busy pathway is packed with cyclists and rollerbladers and no friend to dogs. In the main park are three marked trails, plus miles of unmarked hikes.

TRAIL TIME?
>More than an hour.

TRAIL TERRAIN?
>The Multi-Use Trail is gently sloping across the rolling terrain; the Valley Creek and Schuylkill River Trails are flat, waterside walks. The Horse-Shoe Trail calls for a steep and strenuos climb up Mount Misery, the natural southern defender of Washington's encampment.

TRAIL SURFACE?
>The Multi-Use Trail is paved while the others are dirt trails.

TRAIL SENSE?

A National Park Service map provides locations for the
trails but does not indicate the variety of side trails
available, especially from the Schuylkill River Trail which
leads away from the river on an old Pennsylvania Railroad
grade. Only the Horseshoe Trail is blazed.

SWIMMING?

Valley Creek is a delightful watering hole and the Schuylkill
River is easily accessed for hard-core swimming canines.

ADMISSION FEE:

None.

PARK HOURS/PHONE:

Dawn to dusk. (610.783.1000)

DIRECTIONS:

The main park entrance is on Route 23 off Route 422.
Parking for the Valley Creek Trail is on Route 252
(although the Foot Bridge is washed out as of this writing).
To reach the Schuylkill River Trail, exit from Route 422
onto Trooper Road, make a left and continue back across
Route 422 to the Betzwood Picnic Area or cross the
Schuylkill River on Pawlings Road from Route 23 at the
other end.

Nearby Parks

ANDORRA NATURAL AREA/ FAIRMOUNT PARK

Philadelphia County, Pennsylvania

THE PARK:

America's first public park began with 5 acres in 1812. Today, Fairmount Park is the largest contiguous landscaped municipal park in the world with nearly 9,000 acres. It is home to an estimated 2,500,000 trees.

The Andorra Natural Area, at the park's northern boundary with Montgomery County, evolved from a 19th century nursery. Ownership of the property dates to 1840 when Richard Wistar named it "Andorra" from a Moorish word meaning "hills covered with trees." One of those trees - a massive sycamore - grew right through an enclosed porch in the house of the chief plant propagator of the nursery. The weakening sycamore was cut down in 1981 but the Tree House survives as the Andorra Visitor Center.

WALKS:

The main trail at Andorra is a 20-station Nature hike. There are also a dozen other named trails that branch off this loop. The Forbidden Drive also begins its 7-mile journey along the Wissahickon Creek to the Schuylkill River here. The Forbidden Drive, so-named when it was closed to automobiles in the 1920s, can be shortened by several bridges across the Wissahickon. In addition, there are many blazed trails climbing out of the Wissahickon Gorge from the Forbidden Drive.

TRAIL TIME?
More than an hour.

TRAIL TERRAIN?
The Forbidden Drive is flat; although the climbs out of the
forested Wissahickon Gorge are steep, the trails are
relatively easy walking once the task is completed.

TRAIL SURFACE?
The Forbidden Drive is compacted gravel; the woodland
trails are dirt and rocks.

TRAIL SENSE?
The paths are blazed and a map of Andorra is available.

SWIMMING?
The swimming is excellent in the Wissahickon Creek.

ADMISSION FEE:
None.

PARK HOURS/PHONE:
5:00 a.m. - 1:00 a.m., year-round. (215-685-9285)

DIRECTIONS:
Andorra is on Northwestern Avenue between Ridge Avenue
and Germantown Avenue.

FRENCH CREEK STATE PARK

Chester/Berks Counties

THE PARK:

A wilderness fort once stood on the small stream flowing through these woods which was garrisoned by the French during the French and Indian War and thus "French Creek." The hillsides here were dotted with charcoal hearths throughout the 1800s, fueling the nascent American iron industry. French Creek State Park was originally developed by the federal government during the Depression as a National Park Service Demonstration Area. In 1946, the area was transferred to the Commonwealth of Pennsylvania.

WALKS:

Approximately 40 miles of trails visit every corner of French Creek's 7,339 acres. There are 8 featured hikes of between one and four hours' duration. The marquee walk is the Boone Trail, a six-mile loop connecting all the major attractions of the park. All the walks are heavily forested with hardwoods - keep an eye out for the ruins of the area's charcoal-burning past.

TRAIL TIME?

More than an hour.

TRAIL TERRAIN?

There are many steep sections as you ramble about these wooded hills.

TRAIL SURFACE?

Dirt with frequent rocky stretches, especially on the slopes. Some trails make use of fire roads.

TRAIL SENSE?

All the trails sport distinct colored blazes. A trail map is available and you would be well advised to take it as the trailheads and junctions are not named.

BONUS
Considered by some as the "Orienteering
Capital of North America," French Creek has
developed a permanent self-guided course for
the practioners of the art of map and
compass. You can even challenge your dog's
nose in a wayfinding contest.

SWIMMING?

There is abundant access to two lakes, the 21-acre cold water Scotts Run Lake and the 63-acre Hopewell Lake.

ADMISSION FEE:

None.

PARK HOURS/PHONE:

8:00 a.m. - sunset, year-round. (610.582.9680)

DIRECTIONS:

French Creek State Park is located north of Elverson. From Route 23 take Route 345 North to south entrance of the park on the left. From the Pennsylvania Turnpike the park is 7 miles northeast of the Morgantown Interchange (Exit 22).

Best Parks To
Walk The Dog And
Push The Baby Stroller

1. Norristown Farm Park

2. Valley Forge National Historic Park

3. Riverfront Park

4. Curtis Arboretum

JOHN HEINZ
NATIONAL WILDLIFE REFUGE
AT TINICUM

Philadelphia County, Pennsylvania

THE PARK:

There are more than 500 National Wildlife Refuges in the United States and only Philadelphia and San Francisco offer an urban environmental study. When the Swedes settled here in 1634, Tinicum Marsh measured over 5,700 acres. Three hundred years later the tidal marsh had been reduced to only 200 acres. The routing of I-95 in 1969 threatened to finish off the marsh but, in ironic fact, saved it. Congress authorized the purchase of 1,200 acres in 1972, establishing the Tinicum National Environmental Center and enabling the highway to roar through the area.

WALKS:

You can cover about ten miles of trails here in two major loops. The more attractive of the two is around the Impoundment marsh near the Visitor Contact Station. If you have a patient dog you can pause at the Observation Platform or one of the Observation Blinds and try to identify one of the 288 species of birds seen in the refuge.

The western loop, which begins in Delaware County, leads onto a dike in the middle of the marsh and along the Darby Creek. The trail on the dike is narrow to the point of being overgrown during the spring and summer.

TRAIL TIME?

More than an hour.

TRAIL TERRAIN?

Flat everywhere.

TRAIL SURFACE?

Dirt and grass, with long stretches of gravel road.

TRAIL SENSE?
The trail is not marked nor blazed but there is a map available. It is not detailed and expect to take a detour or two near the Route 420 parking area. Also, when walking along I-95, keep to the highway side of the chain link fence.

SWIMMING?
The Darby Creek is accessible but the fish pulled from these waters are contaminated so you may want to limit water time here.

ADMISSION FEE:
None.

PARK HOURS/PHONE:
8:00 a.m. - sunset, year-round. (215.365.3118)

DIRECTIONS:
Take I-95 North. Take Exit 10, Route 291 (Philadelphia International Airport). At the first light make a left onto Bartram Avenue. At the third light make a left onto 84th Street. At the second light make a left onto Lindbergh Boulevard. Make a right into the refuge just past the stop sign. There is also a parking area on Route 420; take Exit 9B for Route 420 North. The parking area is right there.

PENNYPACK PARK

Philadelphia County, Pennsylvania

THE PARK:

Pennypack Park gets its name from the Lenni-Lenape Indians who hunted and fished along the creek for hundreds of years. The City of Philadelphia established the park in 1905 to insure protection of 1600 acres of woodlands and wetlands.

WALKS:

Pennypackpack Park is the younger, rougher brother to the Wissahickon Gorge. The adventurous can search out miles of little-used side trails, many quite narrow, off the main 18-mile multi-use trail.

TRAIL TIME?

More than an hour.

TRAIL TERRAIN?

The land around the Pennypack Creek is modestly hilly, although you can walk for a long time without noticing it.

TRAIL SURFACE?

The multi-use trail is paved. Most of the side trails are dirt and watch for paw-slicing glass on some trails.

TRAIL SENSE?

Pennypack Park is for the explorer; there are no maps or trail blazes or mapboards, save for the general route of the multi-use trail. Let the dog lead the way.

SWIMMING?

The fall line of the Pennypack Creek is in the park; at the fall line, south of Frankford Avenue, the last set of rapids play out and drop to the level of its final destination, the Delaware River. From the fall line to the Delaware, the Pennypack Creek is a tidal creek and changes from shallow to deep and back again in a twice-repeated daily cycle.

ADMISSION FEE:
 None.

PARK HOURS:
 Dusk to dawn.

DIRECTIONS:
 Pennypack Park is in northeast Philadelphia, stretching
 from the eastern border of Montgomery County almost to
 the Delaware River. Parking is generally available near the
 major north-south cross roads through the park.

*They are superior to human beings as companions.
They do not quarrel or argue with you. They never talk
about themselves but listen to you while you talk about
yourself, and keep an appearnce of being interested in
the conversation.*

 -Jerome K. Jerome

RIDLEY CREEK STATE PARK
Delaware County, Pennsylvania

THE PARK:
Settlement in this area dates back to the 1600s when villages grew around the mills sprinkled along the creeks and streams. Much of the park's 2,606 acres were consolidated in the Jefford's family - their "Hunting Hill" mansion, built in 1914 around a 1789 stone farmhouse, now serves as the park office. The commonwealth of Pennsylvania purchased the property in the 1960s - including 35 historic residences - and the park was dedicated in 1972.

WALKS:
Ridley Creek features 12 miles of hiking on four main trails. The White Trail visits most of the areas of the park and the others intersect this loop trail at many points. At its southern end the Yellow Trail connects with the trails of the adjacent Tyler Arboretum. A 5-mile multi-use loop is shared with bicyclists and joggers. Also, an unmarked trailhead just east of Ridley Creek on Gradyville Road offers one of the longest creekside walks in the area. CAUTION: These heavily wooded trails are narrow in many places and you and the dog will be prime targets for hitchhiking ticks.

TRAIL TIME?
More than an hour.

TRAIL TERRAIN?
Most of the trails wind through rolling woodland and meadows. You will be moving up and down often but only an occasional hardy climb is necessary.

TRAIL SURFACE?
Mostly dirt; the multi-use trail is paved.

TRAIL SENSE?

The trails are blazed and easy to follow, except through the parking areas - keep your eye on the pavement here. A trail map is available.

SWIMMING?

Ridley Creek, while extremely scenic, is a relatively minor feature of hiking at Ridley Creek State Park. It is deep enough for swimming when the trail touches upon it. There are no ponds on the property.

ADMISSION FEE:

None.

PARK HOURS/PHONE:

8 a.m. - sunset, year-round. (610.892.3900)

DIRECTIONS:

The park can be accessed from Route 3, 2.5 miles west of Newtown Square, past the Colonial Pennsylvania Plantation. The park may also be entered from Gradyville Road - east from Route 352 or west from Route 252.

SCOTT ARBORETUM

Delaware County, Pennsylvania

THE PARK:

The 300-acre Swarthmore campus is developed to be an arboretum, established in 1929 as a living memorial to Arthur Hoyt Scott, Class of 1895. The 3,000 different kinds of plants have been chosen as suggestions for the best trees, shrubs, perennials and annuals to use in home gardens in the Delaware Valley.

WALKS:

Several area colleges welcome responsible dog owners - Swarthmore's Scott Arboretum is the best walk. The collections are integrated with the stone buildings of the college which dates to 1864. There are also trails through the 200-acre Crum Woods, where your dog need only be under voice control. You'll find dog water bowls at teh drinking fountains here, too.

TRAIL TIME?

More than an hour.

TRAIL TERRAIN?

The walk around campus is level; Crum Woods is situated on a steep hillside.

TRAIL SURFACE?

All the surfaces on campus are paved. The trails in Crum Woods are mostly dirt but can also be broken macadam and stone.

TRAIL SENSE?

There are no trail markings but a detailed campus map is available.

SWIMMING?

Crum Creek is deep enough to permit canine swimming.

ADMISSION FEE:

None.

PARK HOURS/PHONE:
Dawn to dusk, year-round. (610.328.8025)

DIRECTIONS:
The Scott Arboretum is in Swarthmore on Chester Road
(Route 320) between I-95 and Baltimore Pike. Parking for
the Scott Arboretum is just inside the entrance on College
Road, on the left.

A door is what a dog is perpetually on the wrong side of.
                                        -James Thurber

WELKINWEIR

Chester County, Pennsylvania

THE PARK:

Welkinweir ("where sky meets water") was a foundering farm during the Depression when the property was purchased by Everett and Grace Rodebaugh. The Rodebaughs reintroduced native trees and meadows and constructed a series of ponds in the valley beneath the farmhouse.

In 1964, Everett Rodebaugh founded the Green Valleys Association to protect five watersheds draining 151 square miles of northern Chester County. In 1997 the Rodebaughs conveyed Welkinweir to the Green Valleys Association for use as a headquarters and eduational center.

WALKS:

A woodland trail loops around the 162-acre nature sanctuary, leading through wetlands, ponds, and meadows. The trail through the back of the property can be narrow and overgrown. For longer walks, the Welkinweir trail features a short connector to the Horse-Shoe Trail, which skirts the property on two sides.

TRAIL TIME?

More than one hour.

TRAIL TERRAIN?

This is hilly property, especially in the backstretch of the loop.

TRAIL SURFACE?

Mostly dirt trails through the trees. Some of the meadow trails are shaved stalks which are rough on your pets' paws.

TRAIL SENSE?

The West Trail Entrance begins at the parking lot and the trail is blazed in white. It is not a complete loop and there is a property map available to navigate through the developed areas.

SWIMMING?

Although the West Branch of Beaver Run is not deep enough for doggie dipping, it engorges into several ponds on the property.

ADMISSION FEE:

Adults, 17 and up - $5.00; Youths (4-16) - $3.00.

PARK HOURS/PHONE:

9:00 a.m. - dusk. (610.469.4900)

DIRECTIONS:

Welkinweir is west of Phoenixville. From the intersection of Routes 23 and 100, take Route 100 south for 1.1 miles. Make a right on Prizer Road. Follow for .8 a mile to Welkinweir on the left. The Visitor Entrance is the second of three and is marked by a sign.

Dog. A kind of additional or subidiary Deity designed to catch the overflow and surplus of the world's worship.

-Ambrose Bierce

LYME DISEASE

www.ingramcontent.com/pod-product-compliance
Lightning Source LLC
Chambersburg PA
CBHW060717030426
42337CB00017B/2900